A Crabtree

FARM
ANIMAL FRIENDS
HORSES

AMY CULLIFORD

CRABTREE
Publishing Company
www.crabtreebooks.com

School-to-Home Support for Caregivers and Teachers

This book helps children grow by letting them practice reading. Here are a few guiding questions to help the reader with building his or her comprehension skills. Possible answers appear here in red.

Before Reading:

• What do I think this book is about?
  • *This book is about horses.*
  • *This book is about horses on farms.*

• What do I want to learn about this topic?
  • *I want to learn what horses eat.*
  • *I want to learn what colors a horse can be.*

During Reading:

• I wonder why...
  • *I wonder why people ride horses.*
  • *I wonder why some horses are different colors.*

• What have I learned so far?
  • *I have learned that horses drink water.*
  • *I have learned that horses like to run.*

After Reading:

• What details did I learn about this topic?
  • *I have learned that horses eat grass.*
  • *I have learned that horses like to jump.*

• Read the book again and look for the vocabulary words.
  • *I see the word **drink** on page 6 and the word **grass** on page 8. The other vocabulary words are found on page 14.*

This is a **horse**.

Horses can be black, white, or brown.

All horses **drink** water.

All horses eat **grass**.

People can ride horses.

All horses like to run, jump, and play!

Word List

Sight Words

a	brown	this
all	can	to
and	eat	water
be	is	white
black	like	

Words to Know

drink　　**grass**　　**horse**

31 Words

This is a **horse**.

Horses can be black, white, or brown.

All horses **drink** water.

All horses eat **grass**.

People can ride horses.

All horses like to run, jump, and play!

Written by: Amy Culliford

Designed by: Rhea Wallace

Series Development: James Earley

Proofreader: Kathy Middleton

Educational Consultant: Christina Lemke M.Ed.

Photographs:
Shutterstock: Henk Vrieselaar: cover (tl); Jesus Cervantes: cover (tr); Barry Fowler: cover (b); Kent Weakley: p. 1; James Kirkikis: p. 3, 14; Lillac: p. 4-5; Andrej Kubik: p. 7, 14; Sheeva1: p. 9, 14; RMC42: p. 11; pirita: p. 12

Library and Archives Canada Cataloguing in Publication

Title: Horses / Amy Culliford.
Names: Culliford, Amy, 1992- author.
Description: Series statement: Farm animal friends | "A Crabtree roots book".
Identifiers: Canadiana (print) 2020038256X | Canadiana (ebook) 20200382578 | ISBN 9781427134530 (hardcover) | ISBN 9781427132482 (softcover) | ISBN 9781427132543 (HTML)
Subjects: LCSH: Horses—Juvenile literature.
Classification: LCC SF302 .C85 2021 | DDC j636.1—dc23

Library of Congress Cataloging-in-Publication Data

Names: Culliford, Amy, 1992- author.
Title: Horses / Amy Culliford.
Description: New York : Crabtree Publishing Company, 2021. | Series: Farm animal friends : a Crabtree roots book | Includes index. | Audience: Ages 4-6 | Audience: Grades K-1 | Summary: "Early readers are introduced to horses and life on a farm. Simple sentences accompany engaging pictures"-- Provided by publisher.
Identifiers: LCCN 2020049868 (print) | LCCN 2020049869 (ebook) | ISBN 9781427134530 (hardcover) | ISBN 9781427132482 (paperback) | ISBN 9781427132543 (ebook)
Subjects: LCSH: Horses--Juvenile literature. | Livestock--Juvenile literature.
Classification: LCC SF302 .C85 2021 (print) | LCC SF302 (ebook) | DDC 636.1--dc23
LC record available at https://lccn.loc.gov/2020049868
LC ebook record available at https://lccn.loc.gov/2020049869

Crabtree Publishing Company

www.crabtreebooks.com   1-800-387-7650

Printed in the U.S.A./022021/CG20201130

Published in the United States
Crabtree Publishing
347 Fifth Avenue, Suite 1402-145
New York, NY, 10016

Published in Canada
Crabtree Publishing
616 Welland Ave.
St. Catharines, Ontario L2M 5V6